This book is dedicated to all who find Nature not an adversary to conquer and destroy, but a storehouse of infinite knowledge and experience linking man to all things past and present. They know conserving the natural environment is essential to our future well-being.

D1369338

COLUMBIA RIVER GORGE
THE STORY BEHIND THE SCENERY®

by Roberta Hilbruner

Roberta Hilbruner, a fourth-generation Oregonian, lives in Hood River—the heart of the Columbia River Gorge. An interpreter with the USDA Forest Service since 1976, she directed the interpretive program at historic Timberline Lodge on Mount Hood before moving to the Gorge as Director of Interpretation. In 1992, Roberta was awarded the first National Gifford Pinchot Award for excellence—the highest honor bestowed upon Forest Service interpreters.

*The **Columbia River Gorge National Scenic Area,** bridges the border of Oregon and Washington east of Portland and Vancouver, and reaches from wet western forests to the dry high-desert plateaus at the Deschutes River.*

Front Cover: Balsamroot brightens a Gorge hillside, photo by Kerry Wetzel/Borland Stock Photo. Inside Front Cover: Spray from Multnomah Falls showers visitors on Benson Bridge, photo by Jeff Gnass. Page 1: Stream reflection, photo by Joanne Lotter Gurling. Pages 2/3: The Gorge at sunset, photo by Ray Atkeson/American Landscapes.

Edited by Mary L. Van Camp. Book design by K.C. DenDooven.

Second Printing, 1999

COLUMBIA RIVER GORGE: THE STORY BEHIND THE SCENERY. © 1995 KC PUBLICATIONS, INC.
"The Story Behind the Scenery"; "in pictures... The Continuing Story"; the parallelogram forms and colors within are registered in the U.S. Patent and Trademark Office.
LC 95-76619. ISBN 0-88714-091-2.

*F*lying downriver, Canada geese follow the river path—a path that leads past desert plateaus, misty cliff gardens, and mossy rain forests. A path past 10,000 years of tradition and tremendous change.

The rosy western sky paints Crown Point with the golden glow of a summer sunset. Far below an eagle perches on a bleached snag. Silvery strands of plunging water cascade down steep basalt cliffs. Sailboats moored near Rooster Rock are tiny white dots. Across the river, pastoral fields and farms peacefully checker the landscape while a drawn-out whistle heralds an engine pulling its long train of cargo down the ribbon of track through the Gorge.

This is a story of the past. . . of dramatic geologic events, great natural diversity, and rich cultural heritage. It is a story of the present. . .of relationships between landforms and natural phenomena, nature and people, and between cultures. It is a continuing story of stewardship as we seek to preserve the treasure of the Gorge in a contemporary society with needs of its own. And, it is a story of the future. . . of new patterns yet to be created.

Called the "Jewel on the Crown," Vista House overlooks the Gorge from atop Crown Point, 733 feet above the silvery sea-level river.

*The raging floods released by the broken ice dams
scoured the Gorge, further defining
the box-shaped canyon and creating the eastern scablands
we see today. The greatest of the flood waters
crested at 1,200 feet, east of The Dalles.*

Evolution of a Gorge

Erupting volcanoes, rivers of lava, tortured up-heavals of earth, raging floods and massive land-slides — the creation of the Columbia River Gorge is a tale of cataclysmic geological events.

Geologists tell us that about 40 million years ago the Columbia River flowed south from its origin in Canada's British Columbia over eastern Washington state to turn west in northeast Oregon much as it does today. At that time, the river passed through the Cascade Mountain Range in a wide valley now covered by Mount Hood. Western Oregon was beneath a shallow sea and the great Columbia met the ocean near the present-day city of Salem.

For 20 million years, violent volcanic erup-tions piled layer upon layer of lava, ash, and mudflows, building the Ohanapecosh formation, some of the oldest exposed rocks in the Gorge. The surface of the Ohanapecosh rocks weathered into the deep red, slippery clay seen on the slopes above Stevenson, Washington. But some of its rocks were buried so long they changed into new minerals — colorful, greenish rocks revealed in a highway cutbank east of town.

Millions of years later, repeated mudflows covered the exposed red clay with nearly 1,000

Bathed in the light of late afternoon,
*Gorge islands stand sentinel. Scoured by floods,
the rock has endured the power of the untamed
Columbia and now rests in the placid waters
▼ behind Bonneville Dam.*

STEVE TERRILL

Columns of basalt appear to cascade down ◭
an autumn-colored hillside in a different kind of "waterfall." Basalt is the most common volcanic rock, and is abundant in Oregon and Washington. Its smooth texture is fine-grained and black until weathered into grays, browns, reds, or greens. Most colonnades are hexagonal, but shapes may vary from four to eight-sided columns.

feet of ash, boulders, and cobble gravel, interlaced with beds containing petrified wood and leaves. These volcanic mudflows, called the Eagle Creek formation, are visible in the cliffs beneath Table Mountain and Greenleaf Peak in Washington, along the Historic Columbia River Highway at Eagle Creek and at the bridge across McCord Creek in Oregon.

LAVA FLOWS

About 17 million years ago near the Oregon-Idaho border, fiery floods of lava gushed out of long, deep fractures. The hot and fluid lava covered 60,000 square miles of eastern Washington and northeastern Oregon to form the Columbia River basalt group. Over the next 5 million years, these lava flows changed the course of the Columbia many times, gradually pushing the river north. Each new channel the river cut through one flow of basalt was filled by the next molten flood. Geologists believe that Crown Point was formed from a lava flow that filled an old Columbia River channel about 14 million years ago. One deep, narrow, former channel, parallel to the present Gorge and about three miles south, is intersected by the present Gorge near Bridal Veil, Oregon.

▲ *The Columbia River cut through layer upon layer of lava exposed here in the dry, open landscape of Horsethief Butte. Continued weathering eats away at canyon walls, breaking off basalt that crashes down to pile up in the talus slopes at the foot of the towering cliffs.*

In places, the dense basalt poured into the river and small lakes. When the liquid lava hit water it cooled and a crust quickly formed. Molten lava continued to push against the crust, ballooning it into a pillow shape. When the pressure became too great, the lava burst through the crust and formed a new pillow. Piles of these basalt pillows and layers of columnar and "brickbat" (or entablature) basalt that cooled on dry land surfaces built the towering cliffs of the Gorge.

About 12 million years ago, a final flow of Columbia River basalt partly filled the channel. Then for several million years, annual spring flooding further filled this channel with silts, basalts, quartzite pebbles, schist, granite, and rhyolite which washed downriver from as far away as the Rocky Mountains. During this time, the oceanic plate continued to push under the continental plate buckling the basalt layers into anticlines (ridges) and synclines (basins). This warping and uplifting of the Cascade Range lifted the pebble beds. Today, gravel deposits close to present water level near Hood River rise to 2,000 feet near Bonneville, then descend back to water level at the Sandy River.

Between 4 million and 700,000 years ago, basaltic lava from more than 50 local volcanoes displaced the Columbia River yet again. Lava flows dammed the river several times and pushed the Columbia north to its present position. Evidence of these shield volcanoes can be seen up and down the Gorge. Beacon Rock may be the core of an old volcano. Across from Beacon Rock, the southern half of a severed volcano forms Nesmith Point. Underwood Mountain near Hood River and Mount Zion near Cape Horn are covered by these lavas which probably flowed into the ancestral Columbia River Gorge.

GLACIAL ADVANCES

During the last ice age, approximately 15,000 years ago, glacial advances from British Columbia formed huge glaciers that filled valleys. One glacier blocked the Clarks Fork River

Surrounding ▶ stone weathered away leaving this remnant to tower above the oaks, balsamroot, and lupine near Lyle. Colonnades of basalt indicate lava that cooled at the bottom of a molten flow and cracked into vertical columns. Lava that cooled at the top of the flow usually formed the jumbled "brickbat" entablature basalt. The repeating patterns of columnar and brickbat basalt separate different flows of lava.

CRAIG TUTTLE

near Sandpoint, Idaho, and an immense glacial lake (Lake Missoula) filled to cover 3,000 square miles behind the 2,500-foot-high ice dam.

When the water was 2,000 feet deep the ice dam washed away. Water and icebergs swept across eastern Washington and down the Columbia River channel. The glacial ice advanced again and again, reconstructing the dam. Over decades the lake refilled and broke the dam. This process repeated nearly 90 times over a period of 2,000 years.

The raging floods released by the broken ice dams scoured the Gorge, further defining the box-shaped canyon and creating the eastern scablands we see today. The greatest of the flood waters crested at 1,200 feet, east of The Dalles. The

STEVE TERRILL

Laminated layers of lava bared at Shadow ▶ Cove near Viento reveal a story of earth's fabric gently folded. Throughout the Gorge, sloping basalt illustrates the effects of plate tectonics in pointing anticlines and sinking synclines.

RON CRONIN

site of today's Mayer State Park was 200 feet underwater. At Crown Point, the water was 600-700 feet deep — where it might have lapped at the top of this towering cliff. The river continues to erode its canyon, as it has through time. The powerful Columbia, cutting through the layers of basalt faster than its smaller tributaries, left these "hanging streams" behind to plunge over Gorge cliffs in breathtaking waterfalls.

The steep walls of the Gorge, tilted southward, shaken by earthquakes and weakened by erosion, slumped in massive landslides. The largest slide occurred just north of Bonneville Dam when the Eagle Creek formation slid off the slippery red clay at the top of the Ohanapecosh formation. This landslide covered 14 square miles, pushed the river a mile to the south, and formed a dam across the Columbia below present-day Cascade Locks. Indians may have been able to cross the river on this natural dam. They remember this crossing in legends about the "Bridge of the Gods." When the lake behind the earth dam filled, the dam washed away, leaving the rapids known as the "Cascades of the Columbia" (now drowned behind Bonneville Dam). The final act has still not ended today! Current geologic activity called "landslide creep" can be seen in the active slide between Wind Mountain and Dog Mountain where the highway and railroad need frequent repairs to keep up with the moving earth.

Dramatic geologic events shaped the structure of the Gorge. Weather, wildlife, vegetation, and people have all been affected by the geologic framework of the river's corridor.

SUGGESTED READING

ALLEN, JOHN ELIOT. *The Magnificent Gateway.* Forest Grove, Oregon: Timber Press, 1979.

ALLEN, JOHN ELIOT, MARJORIE BURNS, and SAM C. SARGENT. *Cataclysms on the Columbia.* Forest Grove, Oregon: Timber Press, 1986.

WILLIAMS, IRA A. *Geologic History of the Columbia River Gorge.* Portland: Oregon Historical Society Press, 1991. (Originally published by Oregon Bureau of Mines and Geology in 1916.)

◀ **Starvation Falls plummets down 186 feet of** moss-covered, columnar cliffs. On December 18, 1884, the Pacific Express plowed into a 25-foot snowdrift here as it chugged toward Portland. Holiday passengers were stranded for three weeks. Although no one died, food was scarce, giving the waterfall its name.

▲ **Wind Mountain, intrusive root of a Pliocene** *volcano, sits on the Washington shore opposite its unseen Oregon twin, Shellrock Mountain.*

▲ **A** *natural arch above Horsetail Falls frames distant St. Peter's Dome, an erosional remnant towering 1,500 feet above the river. The pinnacle is constructed of at least six distinctly seen lava flows.*

F*orty million years of cataclysmic geologic history are recorded in the walls of the Columbia River Gorge.*
▼ *The silent stone reveals a visual tale to those who seek the secrets hidden between the giant bookend cliffs.*

CRAIG TUTTLE

▲ ***A** railed path leads hikers past poison oak, penstemon, and August bluebells to a magnificent view* atop 848-foot Beacon Rock. This andesite plug was once the central neck of a former volcano which has been worn away by the river's erosion. Columbia River basalt is, in most cases, a crumbly, unstable climbing medium, but Beacon Rock is one of three Gorge locations favored by climbers. The high quality rock on the south face offers more than 60 routes of varied difficulty. These routes are closed during nesting season to accommodate a pair of peregrine falcons.

◄ **Wahkeena Creek splits and rejoins to form** Necktie Falls which tumbles nearly 50 feet down fern-laden cliffs just off the steep trail above Wahkeena Falls and picnic ground. The Oregon cliffs of the Columbia River Gorge are a waterfall lover's paradise where there are 77 recognized waterfalls within about 420 square miles.

Cascading droplets water a mossy rock ▶ garden along Eagle Creek Trail. Eleven waterfalls within a 3.5-mile walk (7 miles round-trip) make Eagle Creek one of the most scenic canyons and most popular hikes in the Northwest. However, the trail is very exposed along high cliffs and is not recommended for children or for those uncomfortable in high places.

A rich and unusual diversity of plants and animals has been born of the marriage between great variations in moisture and the landforms left by geologic events. The Columbia River travels through one of the few east-west canyons in the world.

Nature's Dazzling Mosaic

The unique geology and climate of the Columbia River Gorge create stunning patterns on a spectacular landscape — lush western rain forests, marshy wetlands, specialized cliff communities, open pine-oak woodlands, and arid eastern savannas.

▲ **Curtains of mosses and lichens drape from** vine maples deep in the rain shadow west of the Cascade Mountains.

A rich and unusual diversity of plants and animals has been born of the marriage between great variations in moisture and the landforms left by geologic events. The Columbia River travels through one of the few east-west canyons in the world. It flows from the arid eastern side of the Cascade Mountains to wet, western slopes where the mountains trap moisture-rich air blowing in from the Pacific Ocean. Before these air masses move to the east they drop an average of 72 inches of rain each year in Cascade Locks, and over 100 inches along the Wind River in Washington. The few clouds that reach The Dalles are only able to generate about 12 inches annual rainfall.

While the river flows by nearly at sea level, Mount Defiance, only four miles to the south, climbs to 4,960 feet. Elevations on both sides of the river reach 3,000 feet, creating a rapid transition from lowland species to subalpine flora and fauna. All this variety in moisture, elevation, and landform adds to the diversity of habitat for plants and animals. Over 800 species of native wildflowers and flowering shrubs bloom here. Fifteen wildflowers and the Larch Mountain Salamander are "endemics" — they exist only in the Columbia River Gorge.

The Gorge supports five major ecosystems: wetlands, western forests, cliffs, pine-oak woods, and grasslands. Although boundaries between ecosystems are not sharply defined, transitions are easily distinguished. From most viewpoints near Hood River you can look west to see dense forest stands and cascading waterfalls. Turning east, the entirely different pattern of pine-oak woodlands is apparent. From atop Rowena

CRAIG TUTTLE

▲ *Brilliant balsamroot (Balsamorhiza deltoidea)*
and blue lupine (Lupinus latifolius) paint the flood-
scoured scablands of Tom McCall Preserve at Rowena
Plateau, managed by the Nature Conservancy. Their
native plant garden at Rowena Crest Overlook
identifies wildflowers of the eastern Gorge.

◀ *Red-winged*
blackbirds are
a common sight,
trilling their
territorial claim
atop wetland
cattails in marshes
throughout
the Gorge.

SCOTT PRICE

Plateau, pine-oak woods are to the west and arid
grasslands fill the eastward view.

WETLANDS

Standing water and seven-foot cattails. Red-
winged blackbirds chucking and scolding.
Dragonflies zipping over the water. Honking
Canada geese. The hidden croak of a western
spotted frog, and the startling rustle of a sharp-
tailed snake slithering through the rushes. This is
a Columbia River wetland.

STEVE TERRILL

◀ **A** *watery ribbon weaves through a wetland* marsh—home to willows, cottonwoods, ash and alders; habitat for tiny fish and frogs; and important rest stop for migrating waterfowl. The wetlands filter pollutants, hold water through dry seasons, and stabilize river shores.

TOM MYERS

▲ **B**lending with gray basalt and silvery water, Great Blue Herons are difficult to spot, but can be found standing at water's edge.

Wood ducks, teals, grebes, coots, and wigeons gabble at each other as they paddle along poking their feathers, adjusting plumage, and nipping at insects. Standing silently on its long legs, a great blue heron turns its graceful neck, cautiously watchful. Common merganser, belted kingfisher, and osprey are regular visitors here and, in winter, snow geese and tundra swans feed on the abundant wapato.

Deer might be seen weaving through the camouflage of black cottonwood, Pacific willow, Oregon white ash, and red alder. A chewed-off willow trunk calls attention to beaver country and a telltale hole in the riverbank signals their den.

The river is well-known to anglers for its chinook, coho, sockeye, and chum salmon runs even though dams, timber harvesting, grazing, and irrigation have taken their toll on habitat. Other fish include bass, walleyed pike, steelhead, chad, and the ancient, enormous, white sturgeon. Sturgeon can live for 200 years and can weigh more than 1,000 pounds!

Fish attract birds like the eagle, osprey,

great blue heron, and kingfisher. Marten, mink, river otter, weasel, raccoon, and striped skunk also prefer homes near the water. Don't forget your binoculars!

WESTERN FORESTS

A magical, enchanting world waits just a step off the highways of the western Gorge. Driving along the Historic Columbia River Highway through a "tree tunnel" of bigleaf maple, voices seem to whisper through the evergreen and call to travelers in the laughing babble of crystal streams. Fairy-tale names identify delicate flowers called fairy slipper, candy flower, queen's cup, toadflax, fairybells, and fleabane.

The steep, forested hills are adorned with swordfern, Oregon grape, Howell's daisy, Columbia kittentails, and salal. A carpet of spongy moss invites a cool rest in a shaded glen. The air is filled with the long, sweet song of a winter wren or the flutelike trill of Swainson's thrush. Those who linger may see flycatchers, red-breasted nuthatches, warblers, and jays.

mammals prefer burrow entrances
beneath rock where they hibernate
more than half the year.

TOM MYERS

Golden maples reach overhead to form a tree
tunnel along the Historic Columbia River Highway.
While autumn brings spots of brilliant color,
over 70 inches of rain keeps western forests
▼ green year-round.

STEVE TERRILL

The brilliant little face of common monkey flower (Mimulus guttatus) greets hikers along cool Wahkeena Creek. This sunny wildflower thrives in the droplets splashed from mountain streams. Like monkey flowers, many Gorge species are found only where it is very wet from misty waterfalls, cliff seeps, or tumbling streams.

RICK SCHAFER/AMERICAN LANDSCAPES

CLIFF GARDENS

Tumbling mountain streams plunge over basalt cliffs in breathtaking cascades of crystal water beads. In winter, freezing temperatures and bone-chilling winds turn these waterfalls into frosty ice sculptures. Water sprayed over cliff faces seeps into cracks, freezes, and breaks off small blocks of basalt. Over thousands of seasons this process has formed bowl-shaped amphitheaters around the waterfalls.

In these misty, rocky bowls and clinging to moist cliffs are the hanging gardens of the Gorge. Mosses, lichens, licorice fern, and maidenhair fern flourish in miniature rock gardens. Botanists believe that the cold climate of past ice ages brought high elevation plants to the Gorge where they still survive on the cool, shaded cliffs. Spreading phlox, lemon-colored desert parsley, and white shooting star are three of these Ice Age relicts.

Many of the endemic Gorge wildflowers, including Oregon bolandra, Barrett's penstemon, and Columbia Gorge daisies, are cliff-dwelling

CHARLES GURCHE

▲ A bit of Oregon Sunshine from the eastern Gorge clings to a fist of soil held in a rocky cleft. Also called golden yarrow (Eriophyllum lanatum).

18

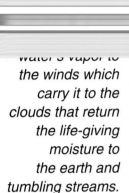

CRAIG TUTTLE

species. One of these, Oregon sullivantia, grows only within reach of a waterfall's spray. Wildflower enthusiasts will find mist maidens, little-leaf montia, Columbia monkey flower, violet suksdorfia, and large-flowered blue-eyed Mary on wet cliffs. Stonecrop, plains mustard, bluebells, western balm, and small-flowered blue-eyed Mary grow on drier outcrops.

The rocky nooks and crannies of the cliffs and steep talus slopes are also home to the tiny pika, a guinea pig-sized member of the rabbit family. Miniature "haystacks" of dried grasses and a squeaky whistle indicate their presence. At the base of the cliffs, a common sight is the comic dipping of the water ouzel as it bobs, dunks, and flips small stones looking for aquatic insects.

PINE-OAK WOODLANDS

Two of the best spots in the Gorge for viewing wildlife and wildflowers are found in the dry, open forests and grassy fields east of Hood River. Between March and June the crest of Rowena Plateau in Oregon and the hillsides sloping down into Catherine Creek east of Bingen, Washington, explode in glorious springtime color.

In April, a rainbow of flowers and panoramic views from Rowena Plateau create a photographer's dream. A path up Catherine Creek winds through ponderosa pine and Oregon white oak. Adventuresome hikers have the option of scrambling up a talus slope through a basalt arch before breaking out onto high, open meadows.

A country road ▷ winds through oak woodlands. These dry, open groves of the middle Gorge ring with the trilling of warblers, and burst into a symphony of color in March and April when glacier lilies and grass widows carpet the forest floor.

STEVE TERRILL

GEORGE WUERTHNER

▲ *Filmy sprays of goatsbeard (Aruncus sylvester),* a member of the rose family, are found nodding sedately at the top of tall stalks in moist woods.

Sunny yellow balsamroot, purple lupine and grass widows, pink shooting stars, creamy orchids, prairie stars and milk vetch, dark-blue larkspur, blue and white camas, and bright, orange-red Indian paintbrush are just a few of the more than 80 varieties of crayon-bright wildflowers found here. Unfortunately, abundant poison oak is also a feature of pine-oak groves!

From tiny warblers to turkey vultures, these park-like woods are teeming with birds hopping amongst the flowers, perching on wind-tossed branches or riding a thermal lift. Western bluebirds, canyon wrens, horned larks, Lewis' woodpeckers, and violet-green swallows are among the species that find refuge in the pines, oaks, and scarce Douglas firs. Springtime finds colorful neotropical warblers resting from migratory flight. At night, screech owls and great horned owls hunt their prey. Terns, gulls, and other water birds crowd the mudflats where the Klickitat River spills into the Columbia.

A warm, summer day in the woodlands might find yellow-bellied marmots sunning on the rocks, badgers scratching for grubs, and mule deer cautiously browsing on acorns. These peaceful pastimes come to an abrupt end when a bobcat slinks onto the scene, or the brittle clatter of a rattlesnake signals a warning to an unwary hiker.

GRASSLANDS

Winds ripple across the grassy savannas of the eastern Gorge in great, golden waves — shaking bitterbrush, mock orange, and rabbitbrush, and tumbling the spiky sage. Magpies nag in nasal tones and a quail family scurries on its way

A stream of spring monkey flowers tumbles  *down a grassy hillside, evidence of moisture in a dry climate. Springtime in the eastern Gorge finds waves of color cascading downhill in areas where water collects. These rolling hills will turn brown and brittle in the summer sun.*

PHOTOS BY STEVE TERRILL

▲ *Yellow flag (Iris pseudacorus) waves its pennant from the edge of a wetland. American Indians once used fibers from the leaf edges of this and other iris species to make strong, pliable cording.*

around an occasional cactus. The sweet, melodious trilling of a meadowlark rises from fields of yellow blanketflower, pea, clover, slender goditia, and baby stars. A spring pond in this arid, treeless country is a bright oasis of purple iris, purslane speedwell, and showy downingia. An April drive up the Dalles Mountain Road is a wildflower lover's delight, and later spring brings treasures hidden in fascinating seed pods of all shapes and sizes.

On milkweed stalks, monarch butterflies transform from chrysalis to fluttering beauty. On top of his mound, a burrowing owl bobs and bows in disturbed agitation. Goldfinches, savannah sparrows, mourning doves, and horned larks are common here, as are the chukars whose loud calls and colorful coveys enliven the savanna scene.

SUGGESTED READING

BURT, WILLIAM H. and RICHARD P. GROSSENHEIDER. *Petersen Field Guides: Mammals.* Boston: Houghton Mifflin Company, 1980.

HITCHCOCK, C. L. and A. CRONQUIST. *Flora of the Pacific Northwest.* Seattle: University of Washington Press, 1974.

JENSEN, EDWARD C. and CHARLES R. ROSS. *Trees to Know in Oregon.* Corvallis: Oregon State University Extension Service, 1994.

JOLLEY, RUSS. *Wildflowers of the Columbia Gorge.* Portland: Oregon Historical Society Press, 1988.

NEHLS, HARRY B. *Familiar Birds of the Northwest.* Portland: Portland Audubon Society, 1981.

PLUMB GREGORY A. *A Waterfall Lover's Guide to the Pacific Northwest.* Seattle: The Mountaineers, 1989.

Pouring down ▶ from the Columbia Wilderness, the crystalline waters of Eagle Creek ladle into classic Punchbowl Falls, a 2.1-mile walk from the Eagle Creek trailhead.

In 1915, ▶ George Shepperd donated his family place of worship to the State of Oregon, so tiered Shepperd's Dell Falls is now a tiny public park.

◀ ***An exquisite*** watery triplet, aptly named Triple Falls, delights hikers along the Oneonta Trail.

Tanner Creek ▶ thunders over Wahclella Falls and rushes downhill to supply Bonneville Fish Hatchery before joining the Columbia.

▲ *"...sunshine above, cool shadows beneath,*
with only flecks of sunlight on the bottom. The
strained light filtering through painted leaves, as
though through colored windows, produces
a dreamy enchanted atmosphere like that of
some old cathedral."—John Muir

*O**verleaf: McCord Creek freefalls in a* ▶
289-foot unobstructed plunge over Elowah
Falls where autumn litters a mossy carpet with
golden leaves. Photo by Charles Gurche.

23

▲ **Columbia desert parsley (Lomatium columbianum), found** on open slopes of the eastern Gorge, is one of 15 endemic flowers that grow only in the area of the Columbia River.

RON CRONIN

▲ **Endemic Columbia kittentails** (Synthyris stellata) are at home on cliffs and north-facing slopes.

STEVE TERRILL

STEVE TERRILL

▲ **The scarlet cup (Sarcoscypha** coccinea) brightens the moist forest floor.

STEVE TERRILL

◄ **Another endemic, Barrett's penstemon** (Penstemon barrettiae), thrusts its roots deep into rocky cracks, clinging to cliffs on both sides of the Columbia River near Mosier and Lyle. It is also found in rocky areas near Bonneville Dam.

▲ **Striped coral root**
(Corallorhiza striata) is an
almost leafless member of
the orchid family whose
root is really a hard mass
of rhizomes that utilize a
fungus to absorb nutrients
from the forest floor.

High on an eastern Gorge ▲
hillside splashed with
balsamroot, lupine, and Indian
paintbrush, a log "bench"
beneath an Oregon white oak
beckons one to rest and
exult in the glorious beauty
of this special place.

◀ **S**pines 2-3 inches in length
protect the edible, succulent prickly
pear cactus (Opuntia polycantha).
Found east of Lyle, its low
mounds of flattened pods, or stem
joints are festooned with huge,
showy blooms in early June.

***T**estament to Gorge* ▶ *winds, a gnarled ponderosa pine (Pinus ponderosa) clutches onto a stony hillside near Bingen. The most widely distributed of all North American pines, ponderosa normally stands a tall 225 feet—an important timber producer.*

▲ ***O**ily poison oak (Rhus diversiloba)* grows throughout the Gorge, appearing leafy green in summer and golden to fiery scarlet in autumn—best seen from a distance!

◀ ***S**now-white bark helps identify beautiful* aspen groves. The stem, or petiole, of aspen leaves is flattened at right angles to the leaf blade allowing the leaves to flutter in the slightest breeze, giving the tree its name—quaking aspen (Populus tremuloides).

STEVE TERRILL

▲ *Pacific dogwood (Cornus nuttallii) bursts into showy "flower" against the red bark of a ponderosa pine. But what appears to be a blossom is really four special leaves, called bracts, that attract insects to the tiny, green flower where the bracts join. The dogwood's hard wood was once used for skewers and goads called "dags" in old Europe, leading to the original name of "dagwood."*

RON CRONIN

▲ *Northwest forests are cloaked with "fake" firs! True firs have cones that stand upright and fall apart while still on the tree. Douglas-fir (Pseudotsugamenziesii) has hanging cones that fall to the ground intact.*

29

Diversity of Life

The Columbia Gorge is a land of contrasts. The sea-level river flows at the foot of peaks reaching 4,000 feet. Rains of 75 inches per year nourish lush forests only 50 miles from arid grasslands. This combination of contrasts provides habitat for a rich variety of life. Small, efficient forms of deep-rooted plants adapted to the dry east change to leggy extravaganzas of leaf and stem as shaded western flora reaches for the sun. The rocky talus, home of tiny, rabbitlike pikas, is just around the corner from the penthouse roost of an osprey. Some species are so adapted they survive only here. Like the contrasting threads of a loom, life in the Gorge is woven into a rich and colorful tapestry.

Some of the wild ones are abundant. Some are rare. All are where they belong.—Kim Stafford

▲ **A**n eerie and sonorous "hoo, hoo-hoo, HOO HOO" signals the presence of a great horned owl. One of the first birds to nest, it lays its eggs in early January.

Treefrogs have the ability ▶ to do unfroggy things! Large suctionpads at toe-tip allow them to climb vertical surfaces, and their clear, melodious call may come from surprisingly high up. Treefrogs can also change color and pattern.

◀ **C**anada geese have a close-knit family life, remaining together until the new breeding year. Goslings are faithfully guarded by both parents, and the family migrates together—their rich, musical honking floating down as they wing overhead in perfect V-formation.

▲ **Graceful tundra swans winter in the Gorge, feasting on the starchy tubers of wapato (Sagittaria** *latifolia), also a traditional food of American Indians. Euro-American settlers called it "duck potato." The swans usually flock to Franz Lake, a National Wildlife Refuge.*

Salmon, once ▷ *incredibly plentiful in the Columbia, but now seriously depleted in number due to habitat degradation, are an anadromous fish—they spend most of their lives in the ocean, but return to freshwater to spawn.*

◁ **Summer days encourage** *rattlesnakes to come out in the open along the woodland trails. Equipped with a warning device at tail's end, their rattle produces a buzzing sound when alarmed.*

*Summer was a time of fishing, hunting,
gathering, drying, smoking, and storing food.
Winter months were filled with the manufacture of tools,
baskets, and clothing—enlivened by
religious ceremonies, dancing, games, and storytelling.*

Those Who Came Before . . .

People have been attracted to the Columbia River Gorge for thousands of years, drawn by the rich diversity of plant and animal life, abundant fish, and the river's transportation corridor. Threads of clues found in bone spear points, campfire charcoal, ancient milling stones, and projectile points associated with atlatl-propelled darts weave a tale of cultural progression in the Gorge.

The 10,000-year-old story begins with northwest hunters of mammoth, camel, and giant bison. Their descendants in the Gorge gradually moved toward a more broad subsistence base and used more advanced tools. They hunted, gathered, and processed waterfowl, fish, big game, small mammals, and plant foods such as camas, couscous, wapato, and yampah.

Clues from arrow points, decorated mauls, net sinkers, carved beads, pipes, trade goods, and the remains of houses tell us that 2,000 years ago the Gorge supported a complex and thriving culture. In the western Gorge, cedar-plank longhouses sheltered extended families. Clothing was made from processed cedar bark, and huge dugout cedar canoes provided transportation. To the east, people lived in tule mat lodges and wore tanned leather garments. Summer was a time of fishing, hunting, gathering, drying, smoking, and storing food. Winter months were filled with the manufacture of tools, baskets, and clothing — enlivened by religious ceremonies, dancing, games, and storytelling.

This culture was the most sophisticated in the region and the Gorge was the trade center of the Northwest. People came from the plains, the coast, the far north, and the Shasta area to the south. Skins, fish, oil, roots, feathers, clothing, shells, horses, bone beads, canoes, and slaves exchanged hands. Sadly, with trade goods came disease. It was brought first by Indians from far away who had come into early contact with European cultures. Then it came with the explorers themselves.

STEVE TERRILL

▲ *Today's Gorge tribes maintain centuries-old lifeways through fishing, gathering of traditional foods such as roots and berries, and annual ceremonies heralding important occasions including the first foods of spring, namings, and memorials. Here, a dancer celebrates his heritage.*

◄ *"Tsagaglalal"*— She Who Watches— guards other precious and sacred pictographs painted on the bluffs near Horsethief Lake. Much of this ancient Gorge art has been lost, flooded by dams or ruined by vandals. What remains may only be seen on a guided tour, reserved through Horsethief Lake State Park.

EXPLORATION

The first Europeans to explore the Columbia River arrived by sea in the late 18th century. Many nations sailed along the Pacific Coast but did not venture upriver until 1792 when Captain Robert Gray from Boston sailed his ship *Columbia Rediviva* into the river's estuaries. He named the great river for his ship and claimed the territory for the United States. Later that year, British explorer Captain George Vancouver brought his vessels to the mouth of the Columbia and dispatched Lieutenant William Broughton to journey up the river. Broughton and his crew of oarsmen rowed 100 miles upstream in a deck boat to give Mount Hood its name and claim the region for England. The two countries argued over these claims for decades.

Cutting through the Cascade Range, the ▷ Columbia River flows between snowy volcanoes. Called "WyEast" by the first people of the Gorge, Mount Hood (shown here) was renamed for a British Admiral by Lieutenant Broughton of Vancouver's expedition.

▲ **At the west end of the Columbia Gorge, Fort Vancouver was the headquarters of the Hudson's Bay** Company's northwest fur-trading operations. Now it is a National Historic Site where reconstructions, a Visitor Center, and costumed interpreters present the history of this fort and industry that had a significant impact upon the Gorge.

The Columbia River took Meriwether Lewis and William Clark to the Pacific Ocean on their journey to find a convenient cross-continental route to the Northwest. Passing through the Gorge in 1805 and 1806, they named prominent features, drew detailed maps, documented the area's botany, geology and zoology, and painstakingly recorded their contacts with native tribes. Their records are thought to be some of the first descriptions of the lifestyle, art, and traditions of these cultures.

Once the rich resources of the Columbia were "discovered" by Europe, the mouth of the river became an international trade center. Fur traders established Fort Astoria and Fort Vancouver. They traveled through the Gorge exchanging glass beads, kettles, buttons, clothing, firearms, and tools with the natives — forever altering traditional patterns. Infectious diseases were introduced by Europeans to the coastal Indians who carried them up the river. Epidemics swept the Gorge. By the early 1800s more than 90 percent of the native population had been extinguished by smallpox, measles, and other European diseases.

PHOTOS BY STEVE TERRILL

Early scientists also visited the Gorge. In the 1820s Scottish botanist David Douglas was directed by the Royal Horticultural Society of London to study the flora of the Northwest. Known as "Grass Man" by native tribes, he tirelessly collected and documented plant communities of the Gorge. The Douglas-fir is named after him. Physician and ornithologist John Townsend and botanist Thomas Nuttal examined the Gorge in 1834. Townsend, known as "the Bird Chief," recorded information about Northwest birds and provided medical services to the epidemic-ravaged tribes.

SETTLEMENT

The descriptions of abundant fish, fur, timber, and fertile land in journals, letters, and reports drew people seeking new opportunities. Missionaries led the way. In 1836, they established Wascopam Mission in The Dalles. In 1843, some 900 people followed their dreams to Oregon. This trickle became a flood of 3,000 in 1845, and by 1849 approximately 11,500 people had walked the rugged 2,000-mile Oregon Trail.

PHOTOS BY STEVE TERRILL

"Old St. Peter's," built in The Dalles ▷
by the Catholic Church in 1897, is now on the register of National Historic Sites. With its towering Gothic steeple, soaring stamped-metal ceilings, and stained glass windows it is a popular site for weddings heralded by the 533-pound bell.

On a hill above The Dalles, "Pulpit ▷
Rock" marks the spot where Jason Lee and other 1830s missionaries climbed up to preach to large groups of Gorge Indians. Their small Methodist Mission was nearby.

◁ *Ezra Meeker, who traveled the Oregon Trail in 1852, placed this rock in a city park in The Dalles in 1906 to commemorate the end of the overland route. The rock is a surrogate for the old "anchor rock" at the east bank of Mill Creek where immigrants camped before continuing their journey on the Columbia.*

🔺 **Indians have fished the Gorge for thousands** of years, perched on rock outcrops or precarious platforms over Celilo Falls and Five Mile Rapids.

🔺 **Fishermen used dip nets to scoop the** plentiful salmon out of the water as they struggled against the current on their way upriver to spawn, until construction of dams flooded the ancient fishing grounds.

◀ **Today,** established treaties protect the right of Gorge Indians to fish for subsistence. A few traditional platforms may still be seen along the Columbia, White Salmon, Klickitat, and Deschutes rivers.

White floats bobbing in the water 🔺 indicate the presence of nets. Most Indian fishermen now use this method of harvesting salmon. The tribes have been actively working with resource agencies to seek solutions to the depleted salmon runs—even volunteering to cease fishing at times.

Pioneers arrived in The Dalles exhausted and out of supplies to face the rapids and windswept swells of the Columbia. They had to purchase supplies to see them through days of cutting trees and building rafts, or they had to pay for canoe transport down the treacherous river. Their journals tell of exorbitant prices, cold, wet, and windy travel, and often relate tales of terror and tragedy on the river.

Conflicts grew between the settlers and the Indians. Forts were established at The Dalles and at the Cascades of the Columbia (the rapids that required portage near present-day Cascade Locks). The disruption of centuries-old lifeways by the diseases, trade goods, customs, and demands of explorers, fur traders, and settlers was profound. The effects on social structure and cultural traditions created tensions which ultimately erupted in warfare in 1856. Although the tribes were eventually relocated to reservations, they retain specific rights to this day, including the rights to gather ceremonial foods and fish the Columbia River.

DEVELOPMENT

The decade of the 1850s saw the beginning of significant transportation development in the Gorge. Mule-drawn portages around rapids gave way to short-portage railroads. Wood-burning steamboats traveled to and from portage stations. Between 1878 and 1896 the first system of river locks was constructed, allowing ships to navigate the length of the Gorge. By 1882, the south bank of the river was lined with a continuous railway. The northern line was completed in 1908.

Improved transportation accelerated settlement and economic development. The Columbia River became an important shipping route for lumber, livestock, grain, fruit, and vegetables grown and processed in the Columbia Basin. Forests were harvested for timber to fuel steam engines and build communities. Lumber camps were established high on the hills and logs were either floated down flumes or carried by short railways to mills along the river's shores.

Fish wheels and horse seines were devised to scoop incredible catches of salmon and sturgeon from the river. A single wheel could ladle as much as 70,000 pounds of fish in a day. Horse-drawn seines could nearly match that amount in one hour. Canneries were built to process the fish, and Chinese laborers were brought from California to toil in the Gorge. By the 1880s nearly 50 canneries dotted the Columbia. In the 1890s the catch began to decline and fish wheels were completely banned by 1934.

The dry, rolling hills and volcanic soils of the eastern Gorge were ideal for growing wheat, while the fertile, volcanic soils of the mid-Columbia tributaries were perfect for orchard crops. Farms, ranches, and orchards added their squares to the patchwork quilt of legged hills and small communities. Warehouses, granaries, canneries, spur railroads, cold-storage facilities, mills, and other associated industries developed near the railroads and ports from which products could be shipped.

STEVE TERRILL

Spring fever strikes ▶ *with a drive through blossoming orchards. Cherries thrive on arid lands near The Dalles, while fertile Hood River valley and Underwood Mountain are famous for their apples and pears. In fall, fresh apple cider and bins of luscious fruit draw bus loads of tourists to celebrate the harvest.*

◀ **Magnificent** Columbia Gorge Hotel was built in 1921 by Simon Benson to serve motorists along the new Columbia River Highway—first paved highway in the Northwest. Sadly, it closed during the Depression, then served as a retirement home for almost 50 years until it was renovated in the late 1970s. Today, the grand hotel once again serves Gorge tourists.

▲ *In 1915, lumberman-philanthropist Simon Benson purchased 300 acres around Multnomah Falls and donated the land to the city of Portland for a park, which was later transferred to Mount Hood National Forest. Historic Multnomah Falls Lodge was constructed of native stone in 1925.*

Eventually, the increasing demand for electricity and President Franklin D. Roosevelt's depression-era economic programs led to construction of dams and transmission lines, forever changing the flow of the river and the patterns on the land.

A New Era

Road travel into the Gorge remained impossible until 1910 when the gravel-surfaced Evergreen Highway was constructed in Washington state to connect Vancouver with the eastern plateau. In 1915, the Columbia River Highway in Oregon connected Troutdale to Hood River. By 1922, this highway extended to The Dalles and had been paved. The commitment of engineer and designer Samuel C. Lancaster to scenic beauty and environmental integrity led to creation of a masterpiece. With its graceful curves, arched bridges, exquisite stonework, and windowed tunnels, the Columbia River Highway was considered to be an internationally significant feat of engineering.

The growing popularity of the automobile brought a new industry to the Gorge — tourism! Campgrounds, roadhouses, and lodges appeared to accommodate travelers. Eagle Creek Campground, the first USDA Forest Service campground in the nation, opened in 1915. Vista House Observatory was built on top of Crown Point in 1918, followed by Hood River's lavish Columbia Gorge Hotel in 1921 and famous Multnomah Falls Lodge in 1925.

At about the same time, an effort was begun to preserve the natural treasures of the Gorge. Private individuals purchased land, donated it for parks, and urged set-asides of Forest Reserves. Successful as they were, these efforts were piecemeal and did not protect the Gorge as a whole.

In the 1970s, appalled by increasing residential development, clear-cut timber harvesting, commercial development, and loss of agricultural land in the Gorge, a number of organizations joined forces to fight these developments. Formation of a federally protected area was first proposed in 1979. Congress passed the National Scenic Area Act in 1986, which President Ronald Reagan signed into law. The Act was established to protect and enhance the scenic, cultural, natural, and recreational resources of the Gorge, and to protect and support the economy of the Gorge by encouraging growth in existing urban areas and allowing economic development that protects Gorge resources.

The Scenic Area Act formed a partnership between the USDA Forest Service, the Columbia River Gorge Commission (a bi-state entity), the six counties in the Gorge, and four tribal governments. In addition, many private citizens have contributed to the planning efforts of this partnership. Together they will shape the future of this precious Gorge.

PHOTOS BY STEVE TERRILL

▲ *Crowds celebrate the 75th anniversary of Vista House, built during 1916-18. The classic building is faced with ashlar sandstone and crowned with copper. Inside, cool marble welcomes visitors to the grand observatory dedicated to the memory of Oregon Trail emigrants. Today, Vista House is an interpretive center featuring exhibits about the Historic Columbia River Highway.*

SUGGESTED READING

BULLARD, ORAL. *Konapee's Eden: Historic and Scenic Handbook — The Columbia River Gorge*. Beaverton, Oregon: TMS Book Service, 1985.

JONES, PHILIP N. *Columbia River Gorge: A Complete Guide*. Seattle, Washington: The Mountaineers, 1992.

SPRANGER, MICHAEL. *The Columbia Gorge: A Unique American Treasure*. Pullman, Washington: Cooperative Extension, revised 1985.

WILLIAMS, CHUCK. *Bridge of the Gods, Mountains of Fire: A Return to The Columbia Gorge*. New York: Friends of the Earth, 1980.

Skamania Lodge was built in 1992 in the "grand lodge" tradition with massive timbers, native stone, and huge fireplaces. Funded by Skamania County, a private developer, and a federal economic development ▼ *grant, the Lodge exemplifies the partnership of the Columbia River Gorge National Scenic Area.*

Columbia River Highway

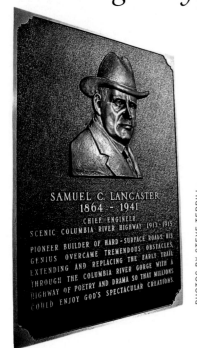

SAMUEL C. LANCASTER
1864 - 1941
CHIEF ENGINEER
SCENIC COLUMBIA RIVER HIGHWAY 1913-1915
PIONEER BUILDER OF HARD-SURFACE ROADS. HIS
GENIUS OVERCAME TREMENDOUS OBSTACLES,
EXTENDING AND REPLACING THE EARLY TRAIL
THROUGH THE COLUMBIA RIVER GORGE WITH A
HIGHWAY OF POETRY AND DRAMA SO THAT MILLIONS
COULD ENJOY GOD'S SPECTACULAR CREATIONS.

PHOTOS BY STEVE TERRILL

▲▼ *The Historic Columbia River Highway melded the practical, a market road, with the romantic—*
exquisite stonework, "eagles nest" observatories, and surprising vistas. Graceful curves hug cliffs, loop down
hillsides, and are reflected by gently arched bridges and stone guard walls. Engineer Samuel C. Lancaster
designed the roadway in harmony with the landscape, "so as not to mar what God had put there." Sadly, the
very demands for good roads that created the beautiful highway also doomed it. By the 1930s, congestion
crowded the important travel route, and speed and efficiency took precedence. In the 1940s, a water-grade
thoroughfare was begun, and much of the beautiful old highway was left to ruin. Today, abandoned sections are
being refurbished for hike and bike paths.

A circle of ▷
arched stonework
allows sightseers a
bird's eye view of the
Gorge as the Historic
Columbia River
Highway loops down
Rowena Crest.
In slower, gentler
days motorists would
stop their Model T's in
the road for a look
over the edge.

STEVE TERRILL

Autumn maples ▷
litter a western curve of the Historic Columbia River Highway. A drive along the winding roadway is a slow-paced, tranquil alternative to the noisy speed of Interstate 84. There is time for peaceful reflection and serene appreciation of the beauty all around—a more intimate opportunity to know the Gorge.

The bridge at Shepperd's Dell is typical of the cast concrete bridges along the Historic Columbia River Highway, where balustrade railings complement graceful arches spanning creeks and canyons. Impressed by the rock windows and arched stone guardrails of the Swiss Axenstrasse tunnel, engineer Sam Lancaster designed the Gorge roadway to emulate the great mountain roads of the European Alps. Look for these arches ▽ *reflected in buildings and publications throughout the Gorge.*

*Threaded side by side through the Gorge
like a string of trade beads,
natural jewels also link us to the past.
The future will bring new patterns.*

Columbia Gorge Today

The Gorge is home to more than 50,000 people. It supports industries, businesses, communities, and farms. Train engines pulling hundreds of cars chug along the river's edge. Tugs push heavily laden barges and tow log rafts up and down the river through its system of locks. Lumber mills process logs, dams crank out electricity, a riverside plant produces and exports aluminum, and Columbia River fruit is internationally acclaimed.

People come from all over the world to drive the Historic Columbia River Highway, to gaze in wonderment at panoramic vistas and breathtaking waterfalls, to hike forested paths, and to raft the wild and scenic rivers that empty into the Columbia. The wind has brought the bright, new colors of windsurfing sails to the Gorge, and tourism has increased economic vitality.

(text continues on page 48)

CHARLIE BORLAND/BORLAND STOCK PHOTO

▲ *From Indian canoes to the 1851 steamboat "James R. Flint," from sail-rigged flat-bottomed barges carrying cordwood to today's sturdy tugs pushing laden barges, the river has served as "highway" and boon to commerce. Here, Mount Hood is backdrop to a tug pushing wood chips to market.*

With the slogan ▷ "Life Begins at 40 Knots windsurfers literally fl across the Columbi River on a "nuclear" day Strong summer wind from the west, an current from the eas combine to creat swells ideal for jump and 360-degree flips catapulting the Gorg into world status among windsurfers. On a typica summer day, hundred of sailors zip acros the water lik colorful butterflies

42

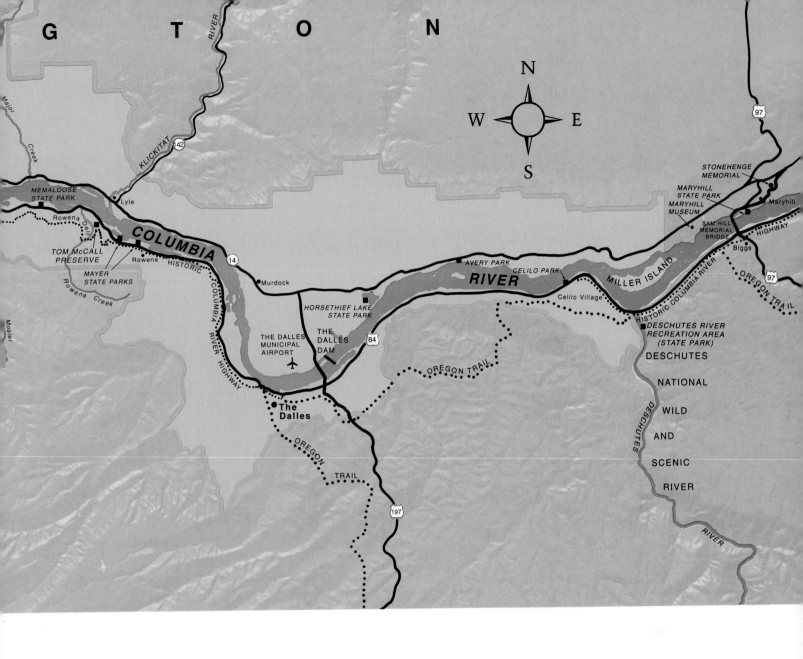

N
W E
S

MEMALOOSE
STATE PARK
Lyle
Rowena Dell
Rowena
TOM McCALL
PRESERVE
MAYER
STATE PARKS
Rowena Creek
Mosier
Major Creek
KLICKITAT
142
RIVER
COLUMBIA
HISTORIC
COLUMBIA
RIVER
HIGHWAY
14
Murdock
THE DALLES
MUNICIPAL
AIRPORT
THE
DALLES
DAM
HORSETHIEF LAKE
STATE PARK
The
Dalles
84
OREGON
TRAIL
197
OREGON TRAIL
AVERY PARK
CELILO PARK
RIVER
Celilo Village
MILLER ISLAND
HISTORIC COLUMBIA RIVER
97
STONEHENGE
MEMORIAL
MARYHILL
STATE PARK
MARYHILL
MUSEUM
SAM HILL
MEMORIAL
BRIDGE
Maryhill
HIGHWAY
Biggs
97
OREGON TRAIL
DESCHUTES RIVER
RECREATION AREA
(STATE PARK)
DESCHUTES
NATIONAL
WILD
AND
SCENIC
RIVER
DESCHUTES
RIVER

TOM MYERS

CRAIG TUTTLE

◄ **S**almon swim upriver through fish ladders
around the Columbia's dams to spawning gravels
in tributary streams. At Bonneville and John Day
dams, underwater windows allow visitors to
get close views of fish and lamprey.

▲ **T**he moon lingers over Sam Hill's re-creation of the
English monument Stonehenge near Maryhill, dedicated in
1918 as a World War I memorial and completed in 1929.

45

*As part of his "New Deal,"
President Franklin D. Roosevelt
approved construction of
Bonneville Dam, one of ten dams
that were planned to tap the
hydroelectric power of the
Columbia River. The Bonneville
project was one of the largest
make-work projects of Roosevelt's
era. Completed in 1938, it put
more than 3,000 men to work
in a depressed economy, and its
product electrified rural areas
of the Northwest. Locks
constructed in association with
the dam provided improved river
navigation.*

*The advent of cheap
electricity drew industry and
contributed to the economic
development of the Northwest.
Bonneville Dam was enlarged
with the north powerhouse in
1983, and new, larger locks were
completed in 1993. Today,
Bonneville Dam still supplies
electricity for the region.
Exhibits in the visitor center
describe the history of the dam,
explain the locks and river
navigation, and explore fish
issues on the Columbia.*

**The released river roars through
floodgates at Bonneville Dam,
where the river's power turns the
giant turbines bringing inexpensive
electricity to the Northwest.**

Columbia Gorge Today

Although change has come to the Gorge, forever altering its patterns, ancient influences can still be seen in the age-old traditions of Gorge tribes. Petroglyphs and pictographs remain to tantalize us with a glimpse into the past. What do they represent? Salmon feasts and root-gathering ceremonies carry on teachings passed through generations. Platforms and dip nets along the river illustrate a culture that has survived devastating events.

Threaded side by side through the Gorge like a string of trade beads, natural jewels also link us to the past. Exotic wildflowers reach back to the Ice Age. Migrating birds return to the Gorge — repeating the timeless, instinctive call of the seasons. Beacon Rock, Cape Horn, Crown Point, and Rowena Plateau illustrate a story 40 million years old.

The future will bring new patterns. The National Scenic Area Act and the resulting Management Plan are an attempt to guide those patterns and protect the Gorge through balancing the needs of a modern society with the treasures of nature and ancient tradition.

▲ *Promise of the future—children frolicking beneath Beacon Rock today will be able to bring the gifts of the preserved Columbia River Gorge to their children in years to come.*

Books on National Park areas in "The Story Behind the Scenery" series are: Acadia, Alcatraz Island, Arches, Badlands, Big Bend, Biscayne, Blue Ridge Parkway, Bryce Canyon, Canyon de Chelly, Canyonlands, Cape Cod, Capitol Reef, Channel Islands, Civil War Parks, Colonial, Crater Lake, Death Valley, Denali, Devils Tower, Dinosaur, Everglades, Fort Clatsop, Gettysburg, Glacier, Glen Canyon-Lake Powell, Grand Canyon, Grand Canyon-North Rim, Grand Teton, Great Basin, Great Smoky Mountains, Haleakalā, Hawai`i Volcanoes, Independence, Jewel Cave, Joshua Tree, Lake Mead-Hoover Dam, Lassen Volcanic, Lincoln Parks, Mammoth Cave, Mesa Verde, Mount Rainier, Mount Rushmore, National Park Service, National Seashores, North Cascades, Olympic, Petrified Forest, Rainbow Bridge, Redwood, Rocky Mountain, Scotty's Castle, Sequoia & Kings Canyon, Shenandoah, Statue of Liberty, Theodore Roosevelt, Virgin Islands, Wind Cave, Yellowstone, Yosemite, Zion.

A companion series on National Park areas is the *"in pictures...The Continuing Story."* This series has **Translation Packages**, providing each title with a complete text both in English and, individually, a second language, German, French, or Japanese. Selected titles in both this series and our other books are available in up to 8 languages.

Additional books in "The Story Behind the Scenery" series are: Annapolis, Big Sur, California Gold Country, California Trail, Colorado Plateau, Columbia River Gorge, Fire: A Force of Nature, Grand Circle Adventure, John Wesley Powell, Kauai, Lake Tahoe, Las Vegas, Lewis & Clark, Monument Valley, Mormon Temple Square, Mormon Trail, Mount St. Helens, Nevada's Red Rock Canyon, Nevada's Valley of Fire, Oregon Trail, Oregon Trail Center, Santa Catalina, Santa Fe Trail, Sharks, Sonoran Desert, U.S. Virgin Islands, Water: A Gift of Nature, Whales.

Call (800-626-9673), fax (702-433-3420), write to the address below, Or visit our web site at www.kcpublications.com

Published by KC Publications, 3245 E. Patrick Ln., Suite A, Las Vegas, NV 89120.

Inside back cover: Sunshine and ▶ *spring storms bring a double rainbow over Crown Point. Photo by Craig Tuttle*

Back cover: Moonrise illuminates ▶ *Crown Point "floating" on a river of fog. Photo by Gary Braasch*

Created, Designed, and Published in the U.S.A.
Ink formulated by Daihan Ink Co., Ltd.
Printed by Doosan Dong-A Co., Ltd., Seoul, Korea
Color Separations by Kedia/Kwang Yang Sa Co., Ltd.
Paper produced exclusively by Hankuk Paper Mfg. Co., Ltd.